D1172507

# Great Ideas of Science

# GENETICS

by Rebecca L. Johnson

Twenty-First Century Books
Minneapolis

*For Dan, the great scientist in my life*

Text copyright © 2006 by Rebecca L. Johnson

All rights reserved. International copyright secured. No part of this book may be reproduced, stored in a retrieval system, or transmitted in any form or by any means—electronic, mechanical, photocopying, recording, or otherwise—without the prior written permission of Twenty-First Century Books, except for the inclusion of brief quotations in an acknowledged review.

Twenty-First Century Books
A division of Lerner Publishing Group
241 First Avenue North
Minneapolis, Minnesota 55401 U.S.A.

Website address: www.lernerbooks.com

Library of Congress Cataloging-in-Publication Data

Johnson, Rebecca L.
    Genetics / by Rebecca L. Johnson.
        p.    cm. — (Great ideas of science)
    Includes bibliographical references and index.
    ISBN-13: 978–0–8225–2910–1 (lib. bdg. : alk. paper)
    ISBN-10: 0–8225–2910–6 (lib. bdg. : alk. paper)
    1. Genetics—Juvenile literature. I. Johnson, Rebecca L. II. Title.
III. Series.
QH437.5.J64  2006
576.5—dc22                                    2004028212

Manufactured in the United States of America
1 2 3 4 5 6 – BP – 11 10 09 08 07 06

# CONTENTS

INTRODUCTION

# BEST IN SHOW

Josh could sense the excitement all around him. But he knew better than to jump or bark or even wag his tail. Josh stood perfectly still as the judge walked slowly past him and the six other contestants. The crowd was silent, waiting and watching. Then suddenly the judge pointed to Josh. The crowd exploded with cheers and applause. Josh had just won Best in Show at the 2004 Westminster Kennel Club Dog Show, the most prestigious dog show in the United States.

Josh is a Newfoundland—Newf for short. That's a very large type, or breed, of dog. A Newf has thick, water-resistant fur, a broad nose, and powerful legs. These dogs are excellent swimmers because they have webbing between their toes, like a duck.

Several hundred years ago, Josh's ancestors were brought from England to Newfoundland, a large island in eastern Canada. Generation after generation, these big dogs were bred for hard work. Their masters wanted them to be strong enough to do everything from hauling wood to helping pull in heavy fishing nets at sea to rescuing unlucky fishers who happened to fall overboard. Despite their huge size, Newfs were also bred to be gentle and sweet tempered. They make wonderful pets and are devoted guardians for small children.

Newfs like Josh are just one of 150 different recognized breeds of dogs. These breeds range from tiny, bug-eyed Chihuahuas and fluffy poodles to speedy greyhounds, shaggy sheepdogs, and towering Great Danes.

How did so many dog breeds come to be? They're all the result of selective breeding. Thousands of years ago, people recognized that certain traits in living things, including dogs and ducks and daffodils, are passed on, or inherited, from generation to generation. At some point long ago, a dog owner mated one of Josh's ancestors—say,

**Thousands of years of selective breeding have brought about many very different dog breeds.**

a big dog with a desirable trait like thick fur—with a dog that had another desirable trait, such as powerful legs. Some of the puppies produced from this mating probably had both thick fur and strong legs. The owner then mated the "best" dogs from this litter with other dogs that had certain desirable traits. Over time, through this careful, controlled breeding process, dog owners developed a new breed of dog, the Newfoundland.

In the same way, selective breeding has resulted in the dozens of other dog breeds. Selective breeding has also given us countless varieties of trees, crops, cattle, horses, cats, birds, and many other living things.

People exhibit inherited traits too. Have you ever heard someone say you have your mom's eyes or your grandfather's dimples? What people mean is that you've obviously inherited certain traits from your ancestors.

Up until the mid-1800s, no one had any idea *how* traits were inherited. Selective breeding was pretty much a trial and error process. People had no scientific way of predicting the outcome of a cross between two particular dogs or horses or corn plants—not, that is, until the 1850s when an Austrian monk named Gregor Mendel decided to conduct some experiments with garden peas. His work laid the foundation for modern genetics and inspired generations of scientists working to unlock the secrets of inheritance.

# CHAPTER 1

# AN AMAZING MONK

Gregor Mendel was born in 1822 in a small village in present-day Czech Republic. His parents were simple farmers who had little money. But Mendel was a good student, and his parents wanted him to make the most of his intellectual talents.

In 1843, at the age of twenty-one, Mendel entered the Augustinian Monastery of Saint Thomas in Brno, also in the Czech Republic. He wasn't all that interested in becoming a priest, but he knew monastic life would allow him to continue his education.

During his first few years at the monastery, Mendel studied agriculture—everything from beekeeping and apple growing to wine making. The monks in charge at the abbey quickly recognized that Mendel had a sharp mind. They sent him to the University of Vienna in Austria. In 1854 Mendel returned to the monastery and taught science at a high school in Brno. He was a very popular teacher.

**From 1856 to 1863, Gregor Mendel cultivated and tracked at least twenty-eight thousand pea plants.**

## PEAS, PLEASE

As Mendel studied and taught and carefully observed the world around him, he became increasingly interested in heredity, or how traits are inherited. In about 1856, Mendel designed a series of experiments to investigate inheritance using ordinary garden peas. Mendel liked to garden, and he had a lot of experience growing peas at the monastery. Besides being easy to grow, garden peas have several traits that are easy to distinguish. For example, the plants are either tall or short. They produce seeds (peas) that are either green or yellow. Mendel could easily track these traits from generation to generation.

Peas are also self-fertilizing. Each flower can make seeds without being fertilized by pollen from another flower. Inside the pea flower petals, pollen from the male part of the flower (stamen) is deposited directly on the female part of the flower (pistil). The contents of the pollen grains combine with tiny eggs at the base of the pistil. These fertilized eggs grow into seeds, which are the peas in a pea pod.

Mendel realized that the self-fertilizing nature of pea flowers made them well suited for heredity experiments.

Why? Mendel could easily cross-pollinate different pea plants. All he had to do was snip off the stamens in one flower, use a brush to collect pollen from another flower, and spread that pollen on the pistil of the first flower. The seeds that formed would be the offspring of the two different plants.

This simple technique allowed Mendel to control which plants—with which traits—became the "parents" of each generation of peas that he grew in his garden. For example, he could take a tall pea plant and fertilize its flowers with pollen from a short pea plant. By analyzing which traits appeared in the offspring of this cross, Mendel was able to track pea plant traits over several generations. Mendel watched closely for patterns in the way traits were inherited, hoping that those patterns would tell him something about heredity.

For the next seven years, Gregor Mendel investigated inherited traits in pea plants. He started with plants that produced offspring with the same traits as their parents, generation after generation. Then Mendel began experimenting. He crossed plants that had different forms

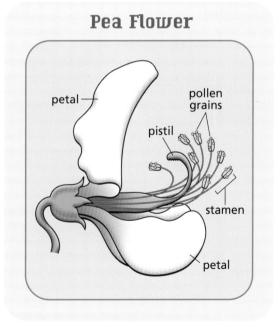

**Pea Flower**

petal

pollen grains

pistil

stamen

petal

of a trait. For example, he crossed plants that produced full pods with plants that produced constricted pods. In a separate experiment, he crossed plants that produced yellow seeds with those that produced green seeds. Mendel did hundreds of crosses and raised thousands of pea plants. He kept meticulous records about all the off-spring of every cross and the traits they exhibited. He examined and counted every pea in every pod produced by all those plants. It's a good thing Mendel liked numbers!

**MENDEL'S OTHER INTERESTS**  Mendel didn't spend all his free time studying peas. He also raised bees, using selective breeding techniques to create better strains of these busy insects.

## UNEXPECTED RESULTS

When he started his experiments, Mendel thought he'd see a blending of traits from one generation to the next. For example, when he crossed a tall pea plant with a short pea plant, he guessed that all the offspring would be medium-height pea plants. Most people in Mendel's day assumed that was how traits were passed on. But that wasn't what Mendel observed. These first-generation plants, as he called them, were all tall. It was as if the short trait had disappeared from the pea population. Or had it?

Mendel let these tall first-generation plants grow and produce seeds. Then he planted those seeds and let them grow into plants. Most of these second-generation plants

**HEREDITY BEFORE MENDEL** People knew the fundamentals of heredity long before Mendel began his experiments. They observed that humans and other animals produce offspring by means of sexual reproduction. They also knew that offspring tend to resemble their parents. For example, farmers who wanted more milk from the next generation of cows were sure to breed their top milk producers. Likewise, farmers who wanted bigger squash planted only the seeds of their largest squash from the previous harvest. These practices are examples of selective breeding.

At this time, however, people did not know how traits are passed from parent to offspring. In about 400 B.C., the Greek philosopher Hippocrates proposed that during intercourse, miniature body parts of the parents (carried by semen in men and a female version of semen in women) joined together in the female, where they developed into a baby. Other philosophers suggested that either the egg or the sperm contained a tiny, fully formed human, called a homunculus. Until the nineteenth and twentieth centuries, scientists simply didn't have microscopes powerful enough to give them a closer look at eggs and sperm.

were tall. But a few were short. The short trait had returned!

Then Mendel noticed something else—something that turned out to be very important. On average, for every three tall plants, there was one short plant. This 3:1 ratio kept appearing again and again in second-generation crosses. It happened for all seven traits Mendel examined. This pattern was too consistent to be just chance. It suggested that some basic law of heredity was at work.

At first, Mendel found his results puzzling. But he had a logical mind and was good at math. He soon figured out what was happening. Each trait he was studying had two forms. For example, the "height trait" was either tall or short. For all seven of the traits he studied, Mendel concluded that each one was controlled by a single factor. Today we call these factors "genes." All of the genes Mendel studied have two forms. One form is *dominant,* while the other form is *recessive.* When the dominant form of a gene is present, it covers up, or masks, the recessive form.

Mendel also realized that in every generation, each offspring (in this case, each pea) inherits one form of the gene for a trait from one parent and one form of the gene from its other parent. So if one of Mendel's peas inherited two dominant forms of the height gene, it would grow up to be tall. If another pea inherited one dominant form and one recessive form, it would still grow up to be tall because the dominant form would mask the expression of the recessive form. But if a third pea inherited two copies of the recessive form, it would be short. In Mendel's second-generation experiments, these combinations were what produced the characteristic 3:1 ratio of tall to short plants.

After eight years of hard work, Gregor Mendel had discovered several fundamental principles that govern heredity.

- Traits are controlled by invisible factors (genes) that are passed from one generation to the next.
- Genes often come in two forms, dominant and recessive.

# Mendel's Peas and Their Traits

| Characteristic | Dominant | Recessive |
|---|---|---|
| shape of ripe seed | round | wrinkled |
| color of pea | yellow | green |
| color of seed coat | gray | white |
| color of unripe pod | green | yellow |
| shape of ripe pod | inflated | constricted |
| position of flowers and pods | axial | terminal |
| height of plant stem | tall | short |

In his experiments, Mendel tracked the inheritance of seven visible traits in garden peas. Each trait has two distinct forms.

- Traits don't blend. The genes that control traits are inherited as individual units from parents. They remain just as distinct in the offspring as they were in the parents.
- Different traits, such as plant height and seed color, are inherited independently of each other.

Mendel presented the results of his experiments at meetings of the Natural Science Society in Brno in 1865. A year later, he published a formal paper with his results and conclusions about how traits are inherited. He sent reprints of his paper to prominent scientists throughout Europe.

Unfortunately, Mendel's paper was largely ignored. There were several possible reasons for this. First, Mendel's results didn't match those of other scientists who were also using plants to try to study heredity. Second, other scientists of that time were not using math to help explain observations in the natural world.

BIG AND SMALL  Mendel discovered that a pea plant receives a gene for height from each parent. That gene may be dominant (D) for tallness or recessive (d). Any plant that receives at least one dominant copy of the gene (DD, dD, or Dd) will grow tall. For this reason, all of the first generation of offspring (F1) are tall. Only a plant that receives two recessive copies of the gene (dd) will not grow tall. On the facing page, the illustration of three generations of pea plants and the chart at the bottom (invented by Reginald Punnett and called a Punnett square) show all possible ways in which the height genes of the F1 plants can combine. It confirms that, on average, for every three tall second-generation (F2) plants produced, one short plant will be produced.

# Three Generations of Traits

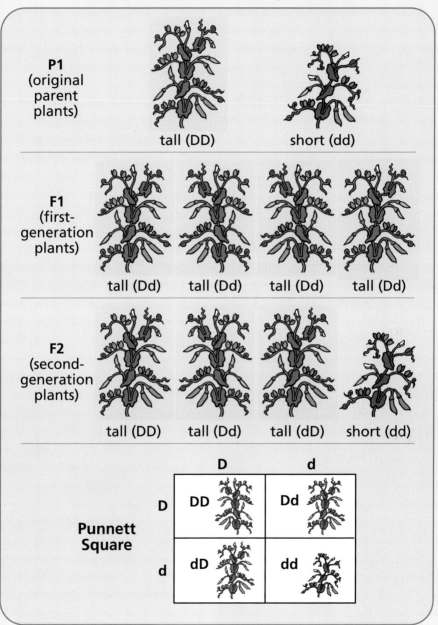

**P1**
(original
parent
plants)

tall (DD)          short (dd)

**F1**
(first-
generation
plants)

tall (Dd)    tall (Dd)    tall (Dd)    tall (Dd)

**F2**
(second-
generation
plants)

tall (DD)    tall (Dd)    tall (dD)    short (dd)

**Punnett
Square**

|   | D | d |
|---|---|---|
| **D** | DD | Dd |
| **d** | dD | dd |

They didn't understand Mendel's ratios. And third, most scientists of Mendel's time focused on things they could actually see in their research. They wanted to know exactly what Mendel's "factors" were. What did they look like? Where were they located? No one, not even Mendel, could answer these questions.

Mendel may have wondered if he'd wasted his time studying peas for so many years. But if he was disappointed with the reception his ideas received, he didn't have a chance to do much about it. In 1868 he was made abbot of the monastery. The responsibilities of this new job took up most of Mendel's time, and he had to give up his research. Gregor Mendel died in 1884 of a kidney disorder. By that time, his paper had been gathering dust in libraries all over Europe for two decades.

# CHAPTER 2

# NATURAL SELECTION AND NEW VIEWS OF LIFE

Around the time Mendel published his paper, most scientists in Europe were preoccupied with other biological hypotheses. An especially revolutionary one had been proposed by two English scientists named Charles Darwin and Alfred Russel Wallace.

In 1831, at the age of twenty-two, Charles Darwin stepped aboard the HMS *Beagle,* an English research ship. Darwin spent the next five years traveling around the world as the ship's naturalist. He approached the task of recording detailed observations and collecting specimens with great enthusiasm.

Darwin had recently finished his studies at Cambridge University in England, where he had been taught that Earth was only about six thousand years old. Scientists of the day generally believed that Earth was changed only by sudden catastrophes, such as the Great Flood described in the Bible. Most people assumed the same kinds of plants and animals had inhabited the planet ever since its creation.

On his journey, Darwin observed many things that made him wonder whether Earth was really so young and so unchanging. While exploring the Andes Mountains in South America, for example, he spotted fossils of ocean animals in rock layers several miles above sea level. How had they gotten there? He found fossils of strange-looking animals that no longer lived on Earth. What had happened to them? Why hadn't they survived?

When the ship stopped at the Galapagos Islands in the Pacific Ocean, Darwin was amazed by the many different kinds of plants and animals he found on the various islands. Each island, for example, had a slightly different kind of tortoise, and none of them resembled tortoises found anywhere else in the world.

Darwin's doubts about the unchanging nature of Earth were reinforced by *Principles of Geology,* a book he read during the voyage. The book's author, Charles Lyell, suggested that Earth was very old and that it had been shaped

These sketches show four different types of finches that Charles Darwin found on the Galapagos Islands. Each bird was especially adapted for the environment of the island on which it lived.

slowly and uniformly by wind, rain, volcanoes, and other forces of nature. If Earth could change slowly over long periods of time, Darwin wondered, why couldn't living things change too? Suppose it had taken millions, not thousands, of years for Earth's landscapes to be molded into their present shape. Wouldn't that be enough time for living things to change—enough time for new kinds, or species, of plants and animals to arise? But how might that happen?

## SURVIVAL OF THE FITTEST

When Darwin returned to England in 1836, he talked with other naturalists about the idea that living things change, or evolve, over time. He pored over his notes from the trip, thinking about what he'd seen. And then, by chance, he read an essay by English economist Thomas Malthus. In studying human populations, Malthus had noticed that when a population grows larger, competition for resources such as food and living space becomes more intense. With greater numbers of people comes a greater chance for disease, famine, and war. In the end, only the fittest members of the population—those with skills or characteristics that help them cope with these challenges—survive.

Darwin applied this idea to populations of animals and plants and other living things. He suspected that any population, from pine trees to pandas, tends to produce more individuals than the environment can support. This leads to a struggle for survival. But which creatures win and which lose this survival game? Darwin reasoned that organisms with inherited traits that help them adapt to their environment would be more likely to survive and reproduce than organisms with less adaptive traits.

As Darwin thought about this, he recalled that individuals within a population are not exactly alike. They vary slightly in all of their traits. In a flash of insight, Darwin realized that this variation was part of the answer he was looking for. Slight variations in an organism's traits might help or hurt its chances of surviving long enough to grow and reproduce—and therefore pass on its traits to its offspring.

Perhaps, Darwin reasoned, the environment "selects" the most adaptive versions of traits, that is, traits that improve chances of survival. Individuals with such adaptive traits will survive to reproduce (and pass on their adaptive traits). Individuals with traits that are not as adaptive die. Over time, more and more members of a population exhibit the adaptive versions of the traits. In this way, the individuals in a population will slowly change.

This gradual change in traits reminded Darwin of selective breeding. People who breed animals or plants artificially select desirable traits they want to pass along to future generations. In time, selective breeding leads to the creation of new breeds and varieties. Darwin believed that "natural selection" was occurring in the natural world. The environment was selecting individuals with traits that helped them survive. And over time, this led to the development of new species of living things.

## SURPRISE AND COMPROMISE

Darwin wrote his ideas down, but he put off making them public for nearly ten years. Finally, just as he was about to publish, he received a letter from another naturalist, Alfred Russel Wallace. While exploring in Malaysia, Wallace had come up with essentially the same idea about natural selection and inherited traits! Darwin could hardly believe it.

After some discussion, the two men agreed to formally present their ideas at the same time in 1858. But since Darwin had the idea first, Wallace insisted he get most of the credit. The next year, Darwin published detailed evidence in support of his ideas in a book called *On the Origin of Species.*

The big unknown in Darwin and Wallace's theory was the way in which natural selection worked. No one, at least no one known in scientific circles, had been able to figure out how traits are passed from one generation to the next. Darwin and his contemporaries also had no idea how variations of traits could arise in a population. They believed that inherited traits were "blended" as they were passed from parents to offspring. They acknowledged, though, that this blending hypothesis didn't really explain all their observations.

Darwin probably would have been excited to learn about Mendel's work. But he never did. Mendel, on the other hand, carefully read *On the Origin of Species.* He even made notes in the margins. Did Mendel realize that his work held the answer to the inheritance question Darwin and others were searching for? We'll never know. What we do know is that throughout the last few decades of the 1800s, many people were trying to understand the puzzle of inherited traits. And Gregor Mendel, who'd already figured it out, was lost in obscurity.

A STORM OF CONTROVERSY    When Charles Darwin published his book, *On the Origin of Species,* it initially caused considerable controversy, especially in religious circles. A few vocal theologians were outraged by the idea that humans were the result of a natural process rather than a special creation by God.

Despite the public controversy, the idea that the diversity of life on Earth is the result of an evolutionary process was accepted almost immediately by most naturalists. Darwin was not the first person to propose the idea that living things change over time. However, Darwin's specific explanation as to *how* that process works—gradual evolution by natural selection—was debated for many years in scientific circles.

## NEW DISCOVERIES

Although the question about inherited traits remained largely unanswered, scientists made several important discoveries about cells during this time. Better microscopes allowed people to examine cells and the tiny structures in them, known as organelles, more closely.

In 1868 Swiss physician Friedrich Miescher was working in a medical research laboratory in Germany. At this time, scientists were just beginning to identify cells' major parts and the kinds of chemicals they contained. Miescher was interested in that cellular chemistry, and he chose to study white blood cells.

Miescher knew of a very good but rather disgusting source of white blood cells: pus from infected sores and wounds. To get the cells he needed for his experiments,

Miescher collected bandages from a nearby hospital. He washed the cells off the bandages and collected them in a beaker. Then he added a chemical that caused the cells to break open. The largest organelle in each cell, the nucleus, was also the heaviest. The nuclei of the broken cells settled to the bottom of the container.

From these nuclei, Miescher extracted a previously unknown chemical substance. He called it nuclein because it came from the nucleus. What Miescher didn't know was that he had isolated deoxyribonucleic acid (DNA), the molecule that carries information about inherited traits.

In 1882 German anatomist Walther Flemming was staining cells with dyes so that their organelles would be easier to see under a microscope. Inside a cell's nucleus, Flemming discovered some strange, threadlike objects that absorbed one of his dyes very readily. These dark-staining structures were chromosomes.

A few years later, Theodor Boveri, who was investigating how chromosomes behave during cell division, noticed that just before a cell divides, its chromosomes seem to disappear. Then—quite remarkably—they reappear in the two daughter cells produced by the division. The chromosomes in these two new cells have the same shape and arrangement as the chromosomes in the parent cell.

Boveri suspected that chromosomes have something to do with inherited traits. When another scientist noticed that different kinds of organisms have different numbers of chromosomes, the link between chromosomes and heredity seemed even stronger. But no one was able to make much sense of all these separate findings.

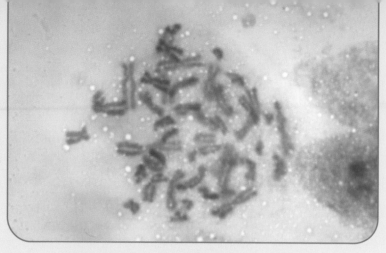

**This microscopic photo shows human chromosomes clustered inside a cell nucleus.**

Nevertheless, the growing interest in chromosomes and cells and inherited traits prompted a flurry of heredity experiments toward the end of the 1800s. Unknown to one another, three European scientists were trying to work out the laws of inheritance by doing crossbreeding experiments with plants. Hugo de Vries conducted experimental crosses with evening primrose plants. Karl Correns studied trait inheritance in corn and peas. And Erich Tschermak von Seysenegg carried out breeding experiments using peas.

By 1900 all three men had reached essentially the same conclusions about inherited traits as Gregor Mendel. As they searched the scientific literature prior to publishing their results, each scientist stumbled across Mendel's long-forgotten paper. Imagine their surprise when they realized they'd simply "rediscovered" Mendel's original findings! Working independently, de Vries, Correns, and Tschermak von Seysenegg confirmed that Gregor Mendel had been right about genes and inherited traits all along.

# CHAPTER 3

# MORE CLUES TO THE INHERITANCE PUZZLE

In the year 1900, the scientific field of genetics—the study of traits and how they are inherited—was truly born. At long last, Mendel was given credit for his findings, and those findings were confirmed and repeated by three other scientists. Using Mendel's basic conclusions about genes and inherited traits, researchers began digging deeper into the question of heredity. What was the hereditary material? Where was it located? And how did it control the inheritance of traits?

Based on observations that had already been made about chromosomes, scientists suspected that chromosomes played a critical role in inheritance. In the early 1900s, chromosomes became the major focus of genetics research.

In 1902 twenty-five-year-old Walter Sutton was a graduate student at Columbia University in New York City. He was studying grasshopper cells, carefully observing their chromosomes, especially during cell division. During one kind of division, mitosis, a cell divides in half to produce two daughter cells. Another special type of division, meiosis, occurs when sex cells divide to produce egg and sperm cells (called gametes).

Sutton noticed that the chromosomes in a grasshopper cell come in different sizes and shapes. But they are identical to the chromosomes in every other

## Types of Cell Division

| Mitosis (division of body cells) | Meiosis (division of sex cells) |
|---|---|
| • a body cell with four chromosomes | • a sex cell with four chromosomes |
| • chromosomes duplicate | • chromosomes duplicate |
| • duplicated chromosomes line up along center of cell | • duplicated chromosomes line up along center of cell |
| • duplicated chromosomes separate; the cell divides | • two duplicated chromosomes move to each side of cell; the cell divides |
| • two body cells, each identical to the original cell and with same number of chromosmes | • each cell undergoes a second division in which duplicated chromosomes separate and the cell divides |
| | • four gametes produced, each with half the number of chromosomes of the original cell |

grasshopper cell he saw under the microscope—except, that is, for grasshopper egg and sperm cells. These cells, which form during meiosis, have exactly half as many chromosomes as all other grasshopper cells. It looked as if sex cells had one set of chromosomes, while all other cells had two.

Sutton quickly grasped the importance of this halving process. It meant that when an egg cell and a sperm cell unite to form a fertilized egg cell, the resulting cell would have the normal number of chromosomes again. It also meant that half the cell's chromosomes would have come from one parent (the father) and half would have come from the other parent (the mother). The link to Mendel's work was unmistakable. Walter Sutton concluded that Mendel's "factors" were contained in chromosomes.

That same year, Theodor Boveri (whom you met in the last chapter) was studying the chromosomes of sea urchins. In one experiment, Boveri noticed a sea urchin egg that had been fertilized by two, rather than just one, sperm. The resulting fertilized egg didn't develop normally. Boveri realized that this doubly fertilized egg had received too many chromosomes. Getting the right number of chromosomes seemed to be essential for normal development.

That observation convinced Boveri that chromosomes are the source of hereditary material. Sutton and Boveri were later credited with taking the first steps in developing *the chromosomal theory of inheritance*—the idea that chromosomes are the source of inherited traits.

## MENDEL MODIFIED

While Sutton and Boveri were examining chromosomes under the microscope, English biologist William Bateson was busy translating Gregor Mendel's paper into English. Bateson was also in the middle of his own experiments on inherited traits. He worked extensively with domesticated fowl, such as chickens. As Bateson read Mendel's paper, he was delighted to discover that the results he was getting in his breeding experiments fit perfectly with Mendel's ideas about how some traits are passed from generation to generation. Bateson became one of the most devoted supporters of Mendel's ideas, and Bateson is even credited with inventing the word *genetics*.

From about 1904 to 1910, Bateson, together with Reginald Punnett, carried out additional breeding experiments. In working with sweet peas, Bateson and Punnett discovered something that Mendel had not. In sweet peas, one gene controls flower color (purple flowers are dominant, and red flowers are recessive) and another gene controls the length of pollen grains (long pollen grains are dominant, and short pollen grains are recessive).

But in breeding experiments, the genes controlling these traits didn't appear to behave independently of one another, as Bateson and Punnett would have expected, according to Mendel's laws. Instead, a surprisingly large percentage of plants with purple flowers also had long pollen grains. By the same token, most plants with red flowers had short pollen grains. Bateson and Punnett suspected that rather than behaving independently, the genes for flower color and pollen length were often being

**A Close Connection** On the surface, linkage initially seemed to contradict Mendel's principle that genes are inherited independently of one another. Eventually scientists discovered that linkage occurs when two genes lie very close to one another on the same chromosome—so close that they are often passed together from parent to offspring.

inherited *together*. It seemed as though these genes were somehow linked, so the phenomenon was called linkage.

Apart from the discovery of linkage, Bateson and Punnett's research confirmed that Mendel's conclusions about inherited traits apply to animals as well as plants. As a result, it seemed logical to extend these laws to human heredity too. In other words, if traits followed a specific pattern in the way they were inherited in chickens and other animals, chances were good that traits were inherited the same way in people.

Obviously, the best way to decipher the details of how traits are inherited in living things was to conduct more experiments. But scientists couldn't very well conduct experiments on people. Animals such as chickens weren't good candidates for heredity experiments either because they grew and reproduced too slowly. For genetics research, scientists needed a small animal that reproduced very quickly and had specific traits that were easy to observe and track from one generation to the next.

## Fabulous Flies

The ideal experimental organism turned out to be the common fruit fly. Fruit flies can produce a new generation every two weeks. Like Mendel's peas, fruit flies have many traits that come in two distinctive forms, such as small or big wings. Better still, fruit flies don't take up much space. They can be raised by the thousands in a lab.

American biologist Thomas Hunt Morgan pioneered the use of fruit flies in genetics research. Morgan thought he could use fruit flies to study genetic changes, or variations, over time.

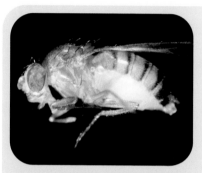

**The scientific name of the fruit fly is *Drosophila melanogaster*.**

In 1910 Morgan set up the "Fly Room" at Columbia University. In these cramped and dusty quarters, Morgan and his students raised countless fruit flies, mostly in small glass milk bottles. The researchers produced generation after generation of flies and carefully examined every one, always on the lookout for something unusual.

After a year, Morgan and his students found what they were looking for. Fruit flies normally have red eyes. But one day, they discovered a newly hatched male fly with white eyes. The researchers had found their first genetic mutation! A mutation is a sudden, random change in a gene. Something had happened somewhere in the genetic material of this fly, causing it to develop white eyes instead of red ones.

Over the next few years, Morgan and his students discovered more than eighty mutations in fruit flies. By exploring how mutations are inherited in these tiny insects, the scientists reached a number of important conclusions. They had no doubt that chromosomes carry all of an organism's genetic information, in the form of genes. They also believed that genes occur in a series on chromosomes, one right after another like beads in a necklace. Furthermore, they confirmed what Bateson and Punnett had suspected: some genes that lie very close together along the same chromosome tend to be linked and are inherited together, as a unit.

Morgan's team combined what they had learned about linkage with another discovery—when cells divide during meiosis, each pair of chromosomes interlocks and exchanges genes. In every division, the chromosome pairs exchange different genes. As a result, each individual egg or sperm cell contains a mixture of genes that is different from the mixture in any other egg or sperm. This process is called crossing over.

One of Morgan's students, Alfred Sturtevant, determined that the farther apart two genes are on a chromosome, the more frequently they are separated as genes cross over. By the same token, if two genes are very close together on a chromosome, they rarely separate as genes cross over. Using this information, Sturtevant created gene maps that showed where he thought genes lay relative to one another on a chromosome.

# Crossing over during Meiosis

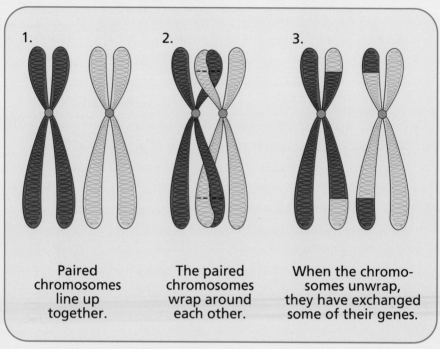

1. Paired chromosomes line up together.

2. The paired chromosomes wrap around each other.

3. When the chromosomes unwrap, they have exchanged some of their genes.

By the 1920s, scientists had gathered considerable data indicating that genes are located on chromosomes. Their experiments had also provided more information about how traits were inherited. But to truly understand genes, scientists had to determine their chemical makeup. It was time to explore the molecular world of heredity.

# CHAPTER 4

# MOLECULAR DETECTIVE WORK

Early chemical analyses of chromosomes showed that they are primarily made of proteins and DNA (what Miescher had found when he discovered nuclein in 1868). Proteins are the building blocks of every cell in your body. Thousands of different kinds exist, ranging from fairly small and simple ones to others that are huge and complex.

In the early 1900s, scientists faced a fundamental question: do proteins or DNA carry information about inherited traits? Many scientists thought DNA molecules were too simple to carry hereditary information. Scientists reasoned that proteins, with all their diversity, were more likely candidates. But several experiments performed on mice and disease-causing bacteria proved scientists wrong.

## ROUGH AND SMOOTH

In 1928 Frederick Griffith was trying to develop a vaccine against pneumonia, a lung disease that is often deadly.

The type of pneumonia Griffith was working with is caused by bacteria.

To develop his vaccine, Griffith began experimenting with solutions that contained killed or weakened bacteria. He tested various mixtures on laboratory mice. Griffith grew two slightly different kinds, or strains, of the pneumonia-causing bacteria in his laboratory. Under the microscope, one strain looked rough on the surface. The other strain looked smooth. Griffith called them the R strain and the S strain to distinguish between the two types.

When Griffith injected healthy mice with the R strain bacteria, the mice didn't get pneumonia. He concluded that the R strain was harmless. Then Griffith did the same experiment using the S strain bacteria. In just a few days, all the mice had died of pneumonia. Blood samples taken from these unfortunate mice were teeming with S strain bacteria.

With the idea of using dead bacteria (which he assumed would be harmless) to create a vaccine, Griffith then killed some S strain bacteria by exposing them to high temperatures. He injected these dead cells into more mice. As Griffith expected, the mice survived and did not get pneumonia. The heat-killed S strain seemed harmless too.

But then, being a thorough scientist, Griffith did one more experiment. He mixed some harmless R strain bacteria with some heat-killed S bacteria and injected this solution in mice. To his surprise, the mice all contracted pneumonia and died a few days later. Stranger still was Griffith's discovery that the blood of these dead mice was full of *live* S strain bacteria! What had happened? Had the dead S strain cells come back to life?

# Results of Griffith's Mouse Experiments

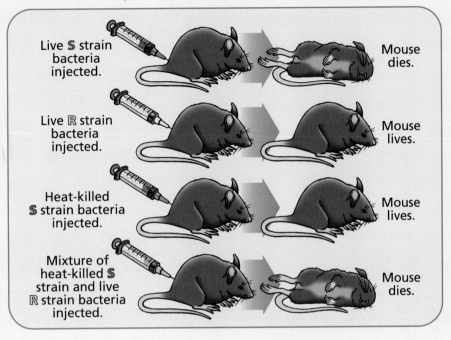

Live **S** strain bacteria injected. → Mouse dies.

Live **R** strain bacteria injected. → Mouse lives.

Heat-killed **S** strain bacteria injected. → Mouse lives.

Mixture of heat-killed **S** strain and live **R** strain bacteria injected. → Mouse dies.

Griffith doubted that was possible. But he did wonder if perhaps the heat had killed the S strain cells but not their hereditary material. Maybe whatever it was inside the S strain cells that could cause an infection had survived the heat treatment and had somehow been transferred to the R strain cells.

After a number of clever experiments, Griffith confirmed this hypothesis. Some mysterious principle had been transferred from the S cells to the R cells, and it had transformed them into disease-causing cells. Even after many generations, these altered bacteria remained infectious, indicating that the change was permanent and inherited.

But what was this mysterious transforming principle?

Monroe County Library System
Monroe, Michigan 48161

In the early 1940s, three biochemists working at the Rockefeller Institute—Oswald Avery, Colin MacLeod, and Maclyn McCarty—carried out experiments using the same two strains of pneumonia-causing bacteria that Griffith had used. Instead of injecting different strains of bacteria into mice, however, these researchers carried out their experiments by mixing the bacteria in test tubes.

First, they used heat to kill S strain cells. They used chemicals to break the dead cells apart, and then they extracted the cells' contents. Next, the researchers mixed this extracted material with harmless R strain cells in a test tube. When the scientists examined the contents of the test tube under a microscope, they found that the harmless R strain bacteria had indeed been transformed into the heat-killed S strain cells into disease-causing S type bacteria.

Next, Avery and his colleagues used different enzymes to selectively destroy different chemical components in the extract from the dead S strain cells. Enzymes are protein molecules that help specific types of chemical reactions take place, such as the breakdown of various chemical compounds. When the scientists added protein-digesting enzymes to the extract, the extract was still able to transform R strain cells into disease-causing cells. But when they added DNA-digesting enzymes, the extract lost its power to transform harmless R strain cells into deadly disease-causing cells. In 1944 Avery and his colleagues concluded on the basis of these experiments that DNA—not protein—is the mysterious transforming principle and is thus the hereditary material.

## Amazing Phages

A few years later, two scientists at Cold Spring Harbor Laboratory on Long Island, New York—Alfred Hershey and Martha Chase—provided more evidence that DNA is the hereditary material but in a very different way. Hershey and Chase were studying a type of virus that infects bacteria. Such viruses are called bacteriophages, or phages for short. Phages, which have a core of DNA surrounded by a protein coat, take over a bacterium's genetic machinery, forcing it to make more viruses.

Hershey and Chase were using bacteriophages known as T2 in their experiments. They knew from electron micrographs—extremely detailed, highly magnified images taken with an electron microscope—that these phages attached themselves by their "tails" to bacteria during infection.

Hershey and Chase assumed that once attached, the viruses inserted their genetic material into the bacteria.

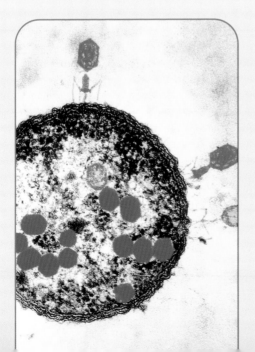

**This electron micrograph shows T2 bacteriophages *(red)* attacking a bacterium called *E. coli.***

The virus genes then "took control" of the bacteria. Information contained in the viral DNA caused the infected cells to stop making bacterial chemical components and start manufacturing the chemical components of new phages instead. Eventually the cells would become so full of new phages that they would rupture. As the cells broke open, the new phages burst out and began searching for more bacteria to infect.

Was phage DNA the substance that exerted this genetic control? Hershey and Chase tried to find out by using radioactive tracers—radioactive compounds that can become incorporated into certain components of cells, such as proteins. Because these compounds emit radioactive particles, their location in a cell can be easily pinpointed. Hershey and Chase "labeled" the protein coat of some phages with one kind of radioactive tracer and the DNA of other phages with a different tracer. Then they added the labeled phages to bacteria samples and recorded where the radioactive tracers ended up. The results were clear. The viruses inserted DNA, not protein, into the bacterial cells. Hershey and Chase concluded that DNA alone carries the instructions needed to replicate phages inside bacteria.

## GENES AND PROTEINS

While many scientists were confirming that DNA was indeed the genetic material, others were exploring how genes control the characteristics of living things. In other words, how genetic information is expressed in the cells of living things.

The first major clue to this genetic puzzle came from work conducted in the early 1900s by an English physician. Archibald Garrod was studying a rare disease called alkaptonuria. The disease seemed to run in families. People who have this disease aren't able to break down, or metabolize, a certain chemical then known as alkapton (homogentisic acid). A clue that a person has this disease is a darkening of urine once it's been exposed to air. Alkaptonuria is fairly easy to spot in infants because their wet diapers turn black. Garrod hypothesized that people with alkaptonuria lack a particular enzyme that is essential to break down alkapton.

Garrod noted that alkaptonuria is inherited in a simple Mendelian fashion (much like the shortness trait in pea plants) and appears to be controlled by a single gene. He suggested that the gene somehow controls the production of the necessary enzyme. People who inherit two recessive copies of the gene can't produce the enzyme and therefore develop the disease.

Nearly forty years passed before Garrod's hypothesis was proven correct. Strangely enough, the confirmation didn't come from studies of human diseases but from two scientists who were studying bread mold!

In the early 1940s, George Beadle and Edward Tatum at Stanford University in California were using X-rays to induce mutations in bread mold. They grew the mold in test tubes on a gelatin-like substance known as growth medium. X-ray treatment produced a number of mutant molds that couldn't grow unless specific nutrients were added to the medium on which the mold was growing.

As the researchers examined each mutant mold, they discovered that it lacked a single enzyme essential for the production of whatever nutrient it lacked.

---

**PERSISTENCE PAYS OFF**    Creating a mutant bread mold wasn't as simple as it might sound. Beadle and Tatum exposed 298 samples of mold to X rays before they came up with a mutant form. That strain, number 299, was able to grow only if they provided it with vitamin $B_6$. At the beginning of the experiment, Beadle and Tatum agreed that if they couldn't come up with a mutant after five thousand tries, they would abandon the project.

---

Based on these experiments, Beadle and Tatum proposed that each gene controls the production of one enzyme (or one protein, since enzymes are proteins). Later experiments showed that the relationship between genes and proteins is a bit more complicated. Some proteins are so big and complex that more than one gene is involved in their production. But the work of Beadle and Tatum confirmed Garrod's idea that a direct link exists between genes and proteins.

So what, you may be wondering, do proteins have to do with inherited traits? Remember that proteins are the building blocks of cells. And cells are the building blocks of tissues, organs, and entire bodies. That means proteins are the raw materials that go into making a flower's colored petals, a snake's scaly skin, a full head of red hair, and all the other physical structures of living things. Scientists kept this in mind as they continued to study genes.

CHAPTER 5

# THE DOUBLE HELIX

By the 1950s, most scientists were convinced that DNA was the material of heredity. They also knew that genes expressed the information they contained by controlling the production of proteins inside cells. But they still didn't know what DNA looks like.

Based on chemical studies, scientists did know the basic chemical components of DNA. DNA molecules are composed of nucleotides. These are chemical building blocks formed by a sugar (deoxyribose), a phosphate, and one of four different nitrogen-containing bases: adenine (A), guanine (G), thymine (T), or cytosine (C).

In about 1950, biochemist Erwin Chargaff and his colleagues at Columbia University began analyzing the base composition of DNA from different kinds of living things. Chargaff was surprised to discover that the base composition of DNA varies from species to species (as you would expect for a substance carrying genetic material). Just as interesting was the pattern Chargaff noticed in the molecule's chemical composition. In every DNA sample Chargaff tested, no matter what kind of organism it came from, *the amount of adenine was always equal to the amount of thymine, and the amount of guanine was always equal to the amount of cytosine.*

## DUELING SCIENTISTS

At King's College in London, England, Maurice Wilkins and Rosalind Franklin were both studying DNA. But they weren't working closely together. In fact, they didn't like each other very much. Franklin was taking "pictures" of DNA using a technique called X-ray diffraction. To produce these pictures, she directed a beam of X-rays at a sample of DNA. When the X-rays struck the DNA molecules, the rays scattered and then struck a photographic plate. On the film, they were recorded as a pattern of spots. The average person wouldn't be able to make much sense of the pictures that resulted from this process. But to someone with a trained eye, a good X-ray diffraction image could reveal a great deal of information about the three-dimensional structure of the molecule.

At Cambridge University, two more researchers were trying to solve the puzzle of DNA's structure. But unlike Franklin and Wilkins, American biologist James Watson and English biophysicist Francis Crick worked very closely together.

An undercurrent of tension and competition ran between the two laboratories. Whoever figured out the structure of DNA first would become instantly famous. Franklin and Wilkins thought using X-ray diffraction to glean clues about the molecule's structure was the best strategy. Watson and Crick, on the other hand, spent their time thinking and talking together about how the known chemical components of DNA might fit together. They were always alert to new information that would fill in the details they didn't know.

In 1952 Franklin produced several exceptionally detailed X-ray diffraction pictures of DNA molecules. Based on the pattern of spots, she and Wilkins were convinced that the DNA molecule is helical. That is, it's shaped like a spiral. They were also able to work out some of the molecule's basic dimensions. Franklin's pictures held all the clues needed to solve the puzzle. But neither she nor Wilkins completely grasped the significance of those clues.

One day Wilkins happened to show one of Franklin's pictures to Francis Crick. Crick instantly recognized the information that he and Watson had been looking for. In a mad rush, he and Watson set to work combining these new details with what they already knew.

Just as Watson and Crick felt they were closing in on a solution, they learned that American chemist Linus Pauling had just published a paper in which he claimed to have determined the structure of DNA. Linus Pauling had previously discovered the helical structure of several protein molecules. And he now proposed that DNA was a triple helix (three strands wound together in a spiral shape).

But as soon as Watson and Crick saw Pauling's "solution," they agreed it couldn't be right. Pauling had forgotten a critical detail—a molecule built according to his model would be chemically flawed and would not hold together. Pauling's mistake spurred Watson and Crick to work even harder. They knew the American scientist would soon realize his mistake and work to correct it.

Watson began playing with cardboard cutouts of the different chemical components of DNA. How *did* they fit together? In a flash of insight, he saw the answer: adenine paired with thymine, and guanine paired with cytosine. This "base pairing" idea explained Chargaff's earlier findings. Watson and Crick brainstormed about how the rest of the molecule's pieces might fit together, and in no time, they had solved the puzzle. DNA consists of two (not three) strands of nucleotides that are twisted together to form a double helix, a shape that resembles a twisted ladder. Two kinds of base pairs form the "rungs" of the molecule: A-T or T-A and C-G or G-C. The sides, or rails, of the ladder are formed by alternating sugar and phosphate groups.

Watson and Crick had figured out the structure of the molecule that carries genetic information in living things. They had taken a huge step forward in understanding the substance that contains the secret of life. Take DNA from any

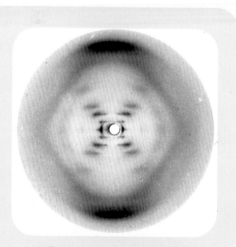

**When Francis Crick saw Rosalind Franklin's Photograph 51 *(above)*, he suddenly understood the structure of DNA.**

organism and the molecule will show the same bonding pattern of base pairs, that is, A with T and C with G. But the sequence of base pairs along the helix—which base pair follows the next along the length of the molecule—is unique for each kind of living thing. How DNA could code for inherited traits suddenly became very clear.

Using metal scraps from the university's machine shop, Watson and Crick built a 6-foot (2-meter), three-dimensional model of DNA. Everyone who saw it agreed they'd gotten it right. Watson and Crick wrote up their results in a short paper, which was published in the scientific journal *Nature* in 1953. Their discovery rocked the scientific world. And it did make them instantly famous.

James Watson *(left)* and Francis Crick *(right)* with their model of a DNA molecule

## DNA Decoded

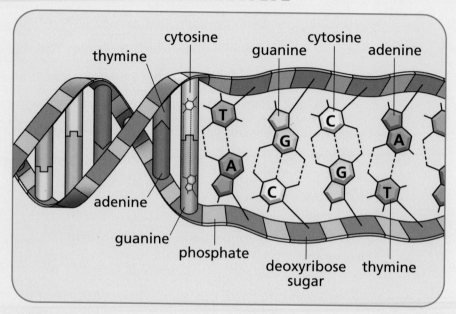

At the end of their paper, Watson and Crick added a simple but enormously important statement: "It hasn't escaped our notice that the specific pairing we have postulated immediately suggests a possible copying mechanism for the genetic material." What did the two scientists mean by this? Not only had they solved the mystery of DNA structure, but they had a pretty good idea how the information in DNA could be copied inside a dividing cell and passed on to the next generation.

CHAPTER 6

# LIFE'S SECRET CODE

The discovery of DNA's structure was a turning point in the history of genetics. Up until that moment, no one could explain how DNA duplicates during cell division so that copies can be passed on to the next generation. The structure of the DNA molecule holds the key to how it copies itself.

DNA is made up of two complementary strands of paired nucleotide bases twisted together to form a double helix. Since A always pairs with T and G always pairs with C, the two strands in DNA are like chemical mirror images. Consequently, both strands contain the same genetic information. And if you think of the two strands as A and B, the A strand can serve as a model, or template, for the B strand, and B can serve as a template for A.

So how does DNA copy itself? Imagine this long, twisted molecule unwinding. As it does, the two strands separate, exposing stretches of nucleotide bases. Inside the cell nucleus are stockpiles of free nucleotides, A, T, G, and C. These free nucleotides begin to pair up with those nucleotide bases exposed along each separated strand. The free nucleotides pair up according to the base pair rule, with As matching up to Ts, and Gs matching up with Cs. As this happens, a new complementary strand is created alongside each original strand and the two strands twist back up into a double helix. Each of the two daughter strands is composed of one original strand and one new strand.

Geneticists call this process DNA replication. DNA replication occurs as a cell is getting ready to divide. It ensures that each of the two new cells receives an exact copy of the parent cell's DNA.

## DNA Replication

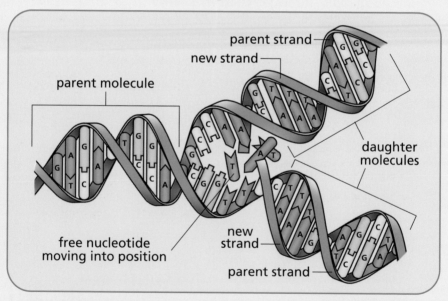

When DNA replicates, or copies itself, the original strands of DNA split apart to generate new complementary strands. The original DNA is known as the parent molecule, and the two new strands—each containing one old strand and one new strand—are called daughter molecules.

# Decoding DNA

Scientists had figured out how DNA copies itself. But they still didn't know how the "messages" stored in DNA are read and expressed as traits in living things. Several researchers had already shown that genes control the production of proteins. Perhaps, they theorized, the sequence of nucleotides in a DNA molecule functions as a sort of code that directs the making of proteins inside a cell.

Scientists made several important discoveries about proteins that helped them connect DNA with protein production. They determined that proteins are made of smaller components, called amino acids. Living things are made up of tens of thousands of different proteins. But all proteins are made from just twenty different amino acids.

So few amino acids can form so many proteins because chains of amino acids link together to make proteins. Each chain folds into a unique shape, depending on the amino acids it contains, to create a unique protein molecule. The great variety of protein molecules in living things results from the sequence in which amino acids are linked together.

How do cells determine the sequence of amino acids needed to make a particular protein? By using the sequence of nucleotide bases in a gene as a guide. After the structure of DNA had been revealed, researchers realized that the genetic code must be a "language" based on the four-letter nucleotide alphabet, A, T, C, and G. Somehow those four letters had to produce enough "words" to

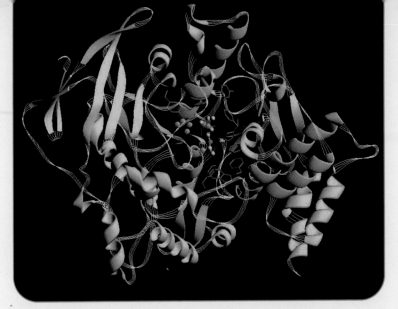

**This computer model is a three-dimensional representation of a protein molecule.**

specify each of the twenty known amino acids. A one-letter code would obviously not work because it could specify only four amino acids, one for each letter. A two-letter code also wouldn't work because it could specify only sixteen amino acids. A three-letter code, however, can produce sixty-four different words—more than enough to code for twenty amino acids.

Marshall Nirenberg showed that the three-nucleotide sequence, AAA, is the genetic code word for the amino acid phenylalanine. Similar experiments revealed more of these code words. Soon, a "dictionary" of three-nucleotide sequences—called codons—had been created for all twenty amino acids. The code had been cracked!

As researchers eventually discovered, many amino acids are specified by several different codons, thus accounting for all sixty-four three-letter combinations that are possible.

A number of codons also act as start and stop signals to mark the beginning or end of a newly built protein.

But how does DNA, which is found mainly in a cell's nucleus, direct protein construction—a process that takes place in the cell's cytoplasm? Scientists discovered that DNA gets help from another nucleic acid found in cells called ribonucleic acid (RNA). RNA is similar to DNA, but the two molecules have important differences. RNA is usually single-stranded, so it looks like one half of a DNA molecule. As indicated by its name, the sugar in RNA is ribose, rather than deoxyribose. Finally, RNA has uracil, instead of thymine, as one of its bases. But like thymine, uracil always pairs with adenine.

## TRANSLATION TO PROTEINS

During the late 1950s and early 1960s, a number of scientists worked out how RNA interacts with DNA to translate the coded information in DNA into the instructions needed to make proteins. Here is what they discovered:

Inside the nucleus, a stretch of DNA that contains the information for building a particular protein unwinds enough so that a complementary strand of RNA can be formed on the exposed bases. The sequence of nucleotides in the DNA segment specifies the sequence of nucleotides in the RNA strand. The resulting RNA strand is called messenger RNA, or mRNA. Messenger RNA is a complementary copy (or transcript) of the coded sequence of nucleotide bases in DNA. It carries a message about the genetic information contained in DNA to the site in the cell where proteins are made.

Messenger RNA slips through the membrane surrounding the nucleus and heads out into the cell's cytoplasm. Its destination is a ribosome, a small, rounded organelle.

The code in mRNA specifies the order of amino acids needed to build a particular protein. These amino acids are already present in the cell's cytoplasm. So are molecules of another type of RNA, called transfer RNA, or tRNA. Individual tRNA molecules have two ends. One end contains an anticodon, a triplet code that is complementary to a particular codon on a strand of mRNA. The other end of a tRNA molecule has an attachment site for a particular amino acid.

Inside the ribosome, the first codon specifying for an amino acid is "read." That amino acid is brought in by a tRNA, which slips into place alongside the mRNA strand. The tRNA anticodon matches up to the codon on the mRNA. Then the next codon is read. A second tRNA arrives with a second amino acid and slips into place. The second amino acid binds to the first one. This is the beginning of an amino acid chain. One by one, the amino acids coded for in the mRNA are brought in by tRNAs and added in the proper order to the growing amino acid chain. Eventually the chain is complete, becoming the protein that the strand of mRNA coded for, which in turn, reflects the code found in the DNA molecule.

The genetic code is truly remarkable in that it is the same in every living thing, from bacteria and fungi to plants and animals—including people. Cracking that code shed new light on how all living things are related and how they are built from the same basic components.

# DNA to Protein

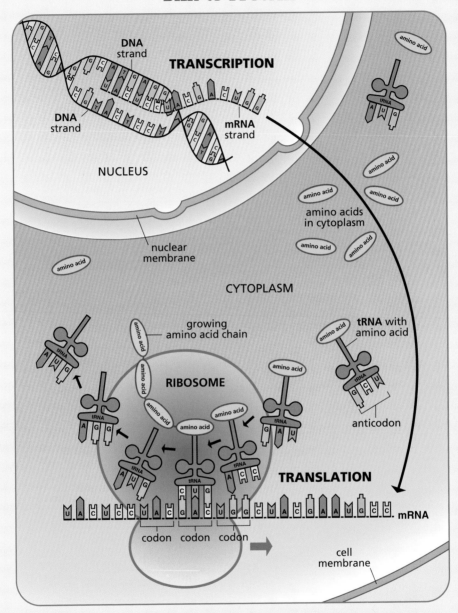

The diagram above shows how the information encoded in DNA, which is located in the cell's nucleus, leads to the creation of a specific protein in the cell's cytoplasm. Two types of RNA—mRNA and tRNA—are essential for this process. The actual creation of a protein, which is made of an amino acid chain, takes place at the ribosome.

## MUTATIONS, GOOD AND BAD

When scientists cracked the genetic code, they learned how to "read" DNA sequences. Each codon, for example, ATG, specifies a particular amino acid. In studying the codons, scientists quickly realized that small errors in DNA sequences could cause big problems. Adding an extra letter along a strand of DNA would change all the codons from that point on. A change in a codon could mean a change in the amino acid incorporated into a protein chain. Such a change could affect the shape and function of the final protein. The bottom line is that even a minor error in the genetic code has the potential to dramatically alter proteins and, therefore, the traits of living things.

Changes in the genetic code are mutations. They can be caused by many things, from exposure to radioactive substances to ultraviolet rays from the sun to viruses.

As you read this page, DNA in millions of cells in your body is being transcribed and translated. On average, scientists think that several thousand errors occur during this process in your cells every day! But you also have about two dozen enzymes that quickly correct these errors.

Sometimes these built-in repair mechanisms fail. As a cell divides, a mutation may be passed on to daughter cells. In this way, it becomes a permanent part of the genetic material in those cells. Some mutations are essentially harmless. Others can be harmful, even life threatening.

But under the right conditions, mutations can also give organisms an advantage. If a positive mutation occurs in egg or sperm cells, it will be passed on to future generations. In this way, mutations lead to variations in living things.

# CHAPTER 7

# THE RISE OF BIOTECHNOLOGY

Once the genetic code was cracked, the pace of genetic research picked up speed. Scientists began pinpointing the exact locations of genes on chromosomes. They explored the details of how those genes work. And they also discovered ways to manipulate genes. Several landmark discoveries—allowing scientists to transfer DNA from one organism to another and to determine the exact sequence of nucleotide bases in DNA—revolutionized genetics. These discoveries opened the door to an entirely new field of research: biotechnology.

## CUT AND PASTE

It all began in 1970, when Hamilton Smith, a scientist at Johns Hopkins University in Baltimore, Maryland, accidentally discovered that when foreign DNA is inserted into a bacterium, the cell chops the "invader" DNA into small pieces. Intrigued, Smith took extracts from these cells and eventually isolated an enzyme that cuts DNA wherever a particular sequence of nucleotides occurs. Smith had discovered the first site-specific restriction enzyme, an enzyme that recognizes and cuts a specific short sequence of DNA.

Not long afterward, scientists discovered other restriction enzymes that could be used like molecular scissors to cut DNA in different places. More than three thousand different restriction enzymes—or restriction endonucleases, as they are also called—have been identified so far. Scientists also discovered another enzyme, called DNA ligase, that can "glue" cut pieces of DNA back together. This amazing tool kit of enzymes for cutting and pasting DNA has had enormous implications for genetic research.

Restriction enzymes and DNA ligase allow researchers to join DNA from different species—to create a new combination of DNA molecules that are not found together naturally. This process is called recombinant DNA technology. Stanley Cohen and Annie Chang of Stanford University and Herbert Boyer of the University of California, San Francisco, were among the first scientists to use restriction enzymes to recombine genes.

In one set of experiments, Cohen and his colleagues fused a segment of DNA that contained a gene from a frog with DNA from the bacterium *E. coli*. They then put the recombined DNA back into an *E. coli* cell. This process of changing an organism's genetic makeup is called genetic engineering.

When the bacterium containing the piece of frog DNA divided, the frog gene was copied and passed on to the resulting daughter cells. When those cells divided, the gene was copied again. Cohen's team had succeeded in cloning the frog gene. Clones are identical copies of an organism, cell, or molecule.

Almost overnight, recombinant DNA and gene-cloning technologies made it possible for scientists to isolate genes from one organism and insert them into the genetic machinery of bacteria. Bacteria can divide very rapidly (every thirty minutes for some species). In a matter of days or even hours, researchers can clone an almost unlimited supply of genes.

## WORKING BACKWARD

At about the same time that some researchers were recombining and cloning genes, Howard Temin and David Baltimore were studying a virus that can cause tumors in chickens. The virus contains only RNA, yet when it infects chicken cells, it is able to take over the cells' machinery, forcing them to manufacture viral proteins. This seemed to contradict the traditional flow of genetic information from DNA to RNA to proteins. What was going on?

Working independently, Temin and Baltimore discovered that when the viral RNA invades the nucleus of a chicken cell, it acts as a template for a strand of DNA that is complementary to the viral RNA. The newly formed DNA joins with the cell's own DNA, and that section of DNA is then translated into mRNA, which travels out into the cytoplasm and controls the assembly of viral proteins. This amazing reverse flow of information, from RNA to DNA, is made possible by a very unusual enzyme called reverse transcriptase.

# RNA to DNA

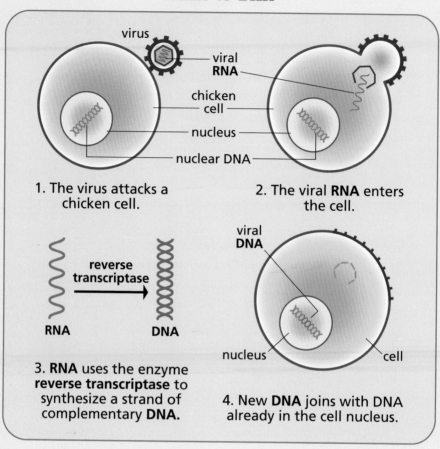

1. The virus attacks a chicken cell.

2. The viral **RNA** enters the cell.

reverse transcriptase

RNA → DNA

3. **RNA** uses the enzyme **reverse transcriptase** to synthesize a strand of complementary **DNA**.

4. New **DNA** joins with DNA already in the cell nucleus.

Reverse transcriptase allows geneticists to "work backward" in trying to identify genes in DNA. Up until its discovery, scientists had only two ways to find a gene: (1) search laboriously through thousands of nucleotide bases for a sequence that codes for the production of a specific protein, or (2) hunt for known sequences that are clues to a gene's location, such as those that represent start and stop points for transcription.

Being able to start with RNA made the old process obsolete. The cytoplasm of a cell is packed with different kinds of mRNA strands that code for specific proteins. By mixing reverse transcriptase with mRNA extracted from a living cell, researchers could quickly figure out the gene that codes for a particular protein's production.

## NEW CREATIONS

One of the first practical applications of recombinant DNA technology came in the late 1970s, when the gene that codes for human insulin (a hormone that helps regulate sugar levels in the blood) was inserted into bacteria. The bacteria were transformed into little insulin-producing factories. In 1982 the U.S. Food and Drug Administration (FDA) approved the sale of genetically engineered insulin.

THE POLYMERASE CHAIN REACTION In 1983 Kary Mullis invented a revolutionary technique for amplifying DNA called PCR, which stands for "polymerase chain reaction." PCR is a superfast method of cloning DNA. Using this technique, it's possible to make *billions* of copies of a specific segment of DNA in just a few hours.

It wasn't long before researchers began inserting genes into more complex organisms. In the 1980s, the first genetically modified mice were developed for use in cancer and acquired immunodeficiency syndrome (AIDS) research.

The timeline starting on page 71 shows other highlights along the road to modern genetically engineered organisms.

Every year the list of genetically engineered, or genetically modified (GM), organisms grows longer. Remarkable advances in technology allow scientists to produce large quantities of rare substances, such as human growth hormone and the natural antiviral agent interferon. Many genetically modified crop plants, such as wheat, cotton, corn, and soybeans, with built-in resistance to certain diseases, pests, and chemicals have been developed. Breakthroughs in research on cancer, AIDS, cystic fibrosis, diabetes, obesity, and many other diseases have been made using genetically modified laboratory animals. You can also thank recombinant DNA technology for many of today's medicines, vaccines, and industrial chemicals.

Genetic engineering has also led to the development of transgenic animals—animals that have one or more genes from a different kind of animal. For example, some dairy goats have had a rat gene inserted to reduce the fat content in their milk. The genetic makeup of "enviropigs" has been altered so that their manure is less of an environmental problem. "Self-healing catfish" have had a moth gene inserted into their DNA, so they can produce an antibacterial protein that protects the fish against infections.

In recent years, some people have begun to criticize the use of recombinant DNA and genetic engineering. Opponents fear that genetically modified foods may not be completely safe to eat. Other critics believe genetically engineered organisms may interact with wild species in

**CLONING** When researchers clone a gene, they produce many identical copies. They can use these copies for several purposes, including gene research and the production of commercially or medically useful proteins. When many people hear the word *clone*, however, they think of something larger than a gene.

A cloned animal is a genetically identical copy of another animal. Animal clones are usually produced by painstakingly removing an egg cell from a female animal, taking out the cell's nucleus, and then replacing it with the nucleus of a body cell from the animal that is being cloned. This altered egg cell is then implanted into the body of a surrogate mother animal (usually of the same species). The egg grows and develops into a copy of its original parent.

In 1996 a lamb named Dolly became the first mammal clone created from the cell of an adult mammal (in this case, a sheep). The list of cloned animals keeps growing all the time. It currently includes pigs, cattle, mules, and cats.

As with other types of genetic engineering technology, cloning is very controversial. Nearly every week, newspapers and television programs include reports about the pros and cons of cloning. This is a field in which new things are happening all the time. So stay tuned!

unexpected ways, with unexpected results. Some people question whether creating transgenic animals is humane. The field of genetic engineering and recombinant DNA technology promises to be a controversial one for some time to come.

# Sequencing Ourselves

DNA sequencing is another major breakthrough that has created new possibilities for genetic scientists. About the time that Stanley Cohen and Herbert Boyer were experimenting with recombinant DNA, another pair of researchers was developing a way to read the pattern of As, Ts, Cs, and Gs in a stretch of DNA. Walter Gilbert and Allan Maxxam at Harvard University in Cambridge, Massachusetts, and Frederick Sanger at Cambridge University devised two different methods for sequencing DNA.

Using DNA sequencing techniques, researchers can determine the exact sequence of nucleotides in any given segment of DNA. And they can do it quickly. In laboratories where DNA sequencing is done, most of the work is carried out by machines and computers.

DNA sequencing also made it possible to create genetic maps that show the size and location of genes on chromosomes. The maps tell scientists how many nucleotide bases a gene contains and in what order they appear. Researchers started by mapping individual, known genes from various organisms. Then they moved on to bigger challenges: sequencing the entire genome of different kinds of living things. A genome is all of an organism's genetic material. It contains the full set of instructions for building and maintaining that organism and passing on those instructions to the next generation.

When scientists first proposed sequencing the human genome, it seemed impossible. But by 1990, the Human Genome Project was under way. It was an international

## DNA FINGERPRINTING

If you watch crime shows on television, you've probably heard of DNA fingerprinting. In 1984 British geneticist Alec Jeffreys developed this technique to identify people by analyzing their DNA.

Although the chemical components in everyone's DNA are the same, the exact order of the base pairs is different for each individual. This unique sequence makes it possible to identify people by their DNA. To do so, all you need are a few cells that have intact nuclei containing DNA. These cells can come from hair, skin, semen, blood—or even spit!

After the DNA is extracted from the cells, it's cut up using restriction enzymes. Small sequences of DNA that vary greatly from one person to the next are cut out and cloned. Then these DNA segments are sequenced. The process produces "pictures" of those sequences that look like patterns of lines. Every person's pattern is unique.

DNA fingerprinting has become a standard practice in forensic medicine, paternity testing, and criminal investigations. A criminal who doesn't leave any actual fingerprints may still leave a trace of DNA that detectives can use to solve the crime.

effort to decode, base by base, all the genes that make up human DNA. Considering that the human genome contains approximately 3.2 billion base pairs, this was a formidable task!

Luckily, shortly after the Human Genome Project began, a new, faster method for sequencing base pairs was invented. Five major institutions from the United States and Great Britain did most of the work, with help from other laboratories in France, Germany, Japan, and China. By 2000 the teams had finished a working draft of the human genome, having sequenced about 85 percent of the total base pairs. Less that a year later, the researchers announced that humans have approximately 30,000 genes. That number was later reduced to between 25,000 and 20,000.

While researchers were sequencing human DNA, other scientists were working on the genomes of smaller organisms. The first of these to have its genome completely sequenced was a bacterium. It has 1.8 million base pairs. A year later, scientists finished sequencing the 12 million base pairs in a cell of baker's yeast (the kind of

**YOUR LUCKY NUMBER** Coiled up inside the nucleus in nearly every cell in your body is about 6 feet (2 m) of DNA. It's twisted and compacted together to form forty-six individual chromosomes, organized into twenty-three pairs. All other healthy people have twenty-three pairs of chromosomes too. It's the characteristic number for our species, *Homo sapiens.* Other organisms have different numbers of chromosomes. For example, mosquitoes have six, fruit flies eight, cats have thirty-eight, and dogs have seventy-eight. Interestingly, although larger organisms tend to have more chromosomes than smaller ones, this is not always the case. A horse has sixty-four chromosomes, while a chicken has seventy-eight, and a goldfish has a whopping ninety-four!

yeast that makes bread rise). Since then the genomes of more than 150 organisms have been sequenced. Studies of these genomes, together with the human genome, have resulted in a new research field: genomics.

What will we learn from our DNA sequence? Scientists hope that after identifying all of our genes, they can begin to better understand how each one functions—and what happens when they malfunction. Researchers have already identified about three thousand inherited human diseases caused by faulty genes. Being able to study these genes firsthand in the laboratory offers great hope for treating and curing diseases. The discovery of cancer genes, for example, has advanced cancer research and treatment options for people with certain kinds of cancer. Researchers hope that similar genetic studies will lead to progress in battling other health problems such as heart disease, AIDS, and genetically related birth defects.

Other areas of genetic research, such as genetic testing and gene therapy, are also expected to make rapid advances as more human genes are identified and analyzed. Genetic testing is a way to screen people for potential genetic problems, such as a disease that might show up later in life. Gene therapy is a technique that involves transferring normal genes for a trait into a person who has inherited faulty genes for that trait. The hope is that the good genes will replace the faulty ones and correct the problem over time.

In 1990 four-year-old Ashanthi DeSilva became the first person to be treated with gene therapy. She suffered

**Ashanthi DeSilva *(right)* and Cynthia Cutshall *(left)* are the first two people ever to receive gene therapy. They both have a rare disease called severe combined immunodeficiency that is caused by a genetic mutation.**

from a rare disorder known as severe combined immunodeficiency, which is caused by a defect in a single gene leading to the absence of an enzyme. As a result, Ashanthi was extremely susceptible to infections. Using gene therapy techniques, doctors transferred healthy copies of the defective gene into some of DeSilva's white blood cells. Then they injected those cells back into her body. They hoped the cells would produce the absent enzyme and create new generations of normal white blood cells. The treated cells did produce the enzyme, but they failed to divide and give rise to new, healthy cells.

Since then, some kinds of gene therapy have become more successful, but there have also been major setbacks. In 1999 an eighteen-year-old boy participating in gene therapy trials died just four days after starting treatment. In 2003 the Food and Drug Administration placed a halt on certain kinds of gene therapy trials after two children undergoing therapy in France developed a leukemia-like condition. Both gene therapy and genetic testing are controversial procedures that raise many ethical questions.

DNA sequencing has also helped reveal relationships among different kinds of living things. Did you know that you share 98.5 percent of your genes with chimpanzees? DNA sequencing has also revealed that every single person (unless that person has an identical twin) has a unique genome. Your genome is different from that of every other person on Earth. In fact, it is different from the genome of every other person who has ever lived!

In April 2003, scientists successfully completed sequencing the entire human genome. It was a great achievement. And it could never have happened without the work and creative ideas of Gregor Mendel, Thomas Hunt Morgan, Rosalind Franklin, and dozens of other researchers.

But in many ways, the sequencing of the human genome is more of a beginning than an end. It is a new starting point for understanding ourselves, our traits, and how we fit into the amazing diversity of life on Earth. Since 2003, researchers have completed sequencing the genomes of the mouse, the chicken, and the fruit fly, and they're working on animals including the kangaroo, the cow, and the domestic cat. In the spring of 2005, the National Human Genome Research Institute announced plans to sequence the genomes of the marmoset, the skate, and the sea slug, along with several insects and fungi. No doubt many more discoveries and surprises lie ahead as a new chapter in the history of heredity and genetics unfolds.

# GLOSSARY

**amino acid:** chemical compounds that are the building blocks of proteins

**anticodon:** a triplet code on a strand of tRNA that is complementary to a particular codon on a strand of mRNA

**bacteriophage:** a virus that infects bacteria, also known as a phage

**biotechnology:** a branch of biology that uses genetic engineering techniques to alter the genetic material of living cells

**chromosome:** a rodlike structure that contains DNA and is located in the nucleus of most cells

**clone:** an identical copy of a molecule, cell, or organism

**codon:** a three-base sequence of DNA that codes for a particular amino acid

**crossing over:** a step during meiosis in which chromosome pairs interlock and exchange genes

**DNA (deoxyribonucleic acid):** the molecule that contains genetic information and is passed from parent to offspring during reproduction. It is shaped like a spiraling ladder and is contained in the nucleus of most cells.

**DNA ligase:** an enzyme that joins complementary fragments of DNA

**DNA polymerase:** an enzyme that assists in generating a complementary strand for a single strand of DNA

**DNA sequencing:** determining the order of base pairs in a strand of DNA

**dominant gene:** a gene that is always expressed

**enzyme:** a protein molecule that makes chemical reactions occur more quickly or efficiently

**evolve:** to change over time

**gene:** a sequence of base pairs located in a particular position in the genome that codes for the production of a specific protein or proteins

**gene therapy:** an experimental procedure to repair damaged genes or replace them with healthy genes

**genetic engineering:** altering genetic material in the laboratory

**genetic map:** a map that gives the precise location of a gene on a chromosome, along with its sequence of base pairs

**genetics:** a branch of biology that deals with how living things inherit physical and behavioral characteristics through the genome and how these inherited characteristics vary from one individual to another

**genome:** all the genetic material in the chromosomes of an organism

**heredity:** the study of inherited traits

**inherit:** to receive genetic material from parents

**linkage:** two genes often inherited together

**meiosis:** division of sex cells to produce egg and sperm cells

**mitosis:** cell division that results in two daughter cells

**mRNA (messenger RNA):** the molecule that carries the complementary sequence of a section of DNA from the nucleus to the ribosome

**mutation:** a random, accidental change in DNA sequence

**natural selection:** the process by which organisms best adapted to a particular environment survive to reproduce and pass on their advantageous genetic traits to their offspring

**nucleotide:** a chemical unit containing a sugar, a phosphate, and a nucleotide base. DNA's four nucleotide bases are adenine (A), thymine (T), cytosine (C), and guanine (G). RNA has uracil (U) in place of thymine as one of its bases.

**organelle:** a structure within a cell

**pistil:** the female reproductive organ of a flower, including the eggs, ovary, style, and stigma

**protein:** a molecule created according to instructions from a gene. Proteins make up cells, tissues, and organs.

**recessive gene:** a gene expressed in an organism only when two copies are present

**recombinant DNA:** artificially joining pieces of DNA from different species

**replication:** the process by which a molecule of DNA generates two daughter molecules before cell division

**restriction enzyme:** an enzyme that cuts apart strands of DNA at a specific point

**reverse transcriptase:** an enzyme that uses the sequence of base pairs in a RNA molecule to build a complementary DNA molecule

**ribosome:** an organelle that assists in bonding amino acids together to form proteins

**RNA (ribonucleic acid):** a molecule similar to DNA that carries genetic information

**selective breeding:** controlled breeding of plants and animals to develop individuals with certain desirable traits

**self-fertilizing:** pollination of a flower by its own pollen

**stamen:** the male reproductive organ of a flower, which contains an anther and a filament and produces pollen

**transcription:** the process of using the DNA sequence to make strands of mRNA

**transgenic:** an organism that contains one or more genes from another species

**translation:** the process of using the mRNA sequence to make chains of amino acids, which fold into proteins. Translation takes place on organelles called ribosomes.

**tRNA (transfer RNA):** a type of RNA that bonds to a specific amino acid and brings it to the ribosome for protein synthesis

**virus:** a disease-causing organism that consists of a small piece of genetic material (DNA or RNA) surrounded by a protein "coat"

# TIMELINE

**1492**    Christopher Columbus makes his first voyage of discovery.

**1658**    Archbishop James Ussher concludes that the Earth was created on October 23, 4004, B.C.

**1831–1836**    Charles Darwin travels around the world aboard the HMS *Beagle.*

**1856**    Gregor Mendel begins experimenting with garden peas.

**1859**    Darwin publishes *On the Origin of Species.*

**1861–1865**    The American Civil War is fought.

**1866**    Mendel publishes the results of his pea experiments.

**1868**    Friedrich Miescher isolates and identifies nuclein (later known as DNA).

**1900**    Hugo de Vries, Karl Correns, and Erich Tschermak von Seysenegg rediscover Mendel's work.

**1909**    Wilhelm Johannsen coins the word "gene."

**1910**    Thomas Hunt Morgan sets up his Fly Room at Columbia University.

**1939**    World War II begins.

**1944**    Oswald Avery, Colin MacLeod, and Maclyn McCarty establish that DNA is the carrier of inherited traits.

**1945**    World War II ends.

**1953**    James Watson and Frances Crick determine the structure of DNA.

**1970**    Hamilton Smith discovers restriction enzymes.

Howard Temin and David Baltimore discover reverse transcriptase.

**1983**   Kary Mullis invents polymerase chain reaction (PCR).

Scientists announce the creation of the first genetically modified plant, a tobacco plant resistant to an antibiotic.

**1984**   Alec Jeffreys develops DNA fingerprinting.

**1988**   The first genetically engineered mouse is licensed for use in cancer research.

**1990**   The Human Genome Project is launched.

Ashanthi DeSilva becomes the first human to be treated with gene therapy.

The first GM cows are created to produce human milk proteins for infant formula.

**1993**   The U.S. Food and Drug Administration (FDA) declares GM food is "not inherently dangerous" and does not require special regulation.

**1994**   The FDA approves the sale of the first GM whole food, Flavr Savr tomatoes, genetically engineered to stay firm longer and resist rotting.

**1997**   The European Union adopts the "Novel Foods Regulation," which requires labeling of foods containing or produced from GM crops.

**2000**   "Golden Rice," a strain of rice genetically modified to be more nutritious, is developed.

**2003**   The Human Genome Project releases the final draft of the DNA sequence for the entire human genome, coinciding with the fiftieth anniversary of Crick and Watson's discovery.

**2004**   Researchers in South Korea announce that they have successfully cloned human embryos.

**2005**   The National Human Genome Research Institute announces plans to sequence the genomes of the marmoset, the skate, and the sea slug.

# Biographies

**WILLIAM BATESON (1861–1926)** English biologist William Bateson became one of the strongest supporters of Mendel's ideas when Mendel's paper on heredity was rediscovered in 1900. Bateson actually coined the term "genetics," and attracted many gifted students to his laboratory, including Reginald Punnett. Bateson demonstrated that Mendel's principles of inheritance are as true in animals as they are in plants. He also discovered the tendency for some characteristics to be inherited together. Unlike most of his contemporaries, however, Bateson didn't support the chromosomal theory of inheritance and the fact that genes were actual, physical structures that controlled heredity. Instead, Bateson believed that traits were passed on by "vibrations" or "waves" that affected the development of an entire organism.

**FRANCIS H. C. CRICK (1916–2004)** English geneticist Francis Crick was a gifted child who read all the books he could get his hands on. He studied physics at University College in London. During World War II (1939–1945), Crick interrupted his studies to serve in the military. After the war, however, Crick settled on studying the life sciences. In 1951 he met James Watson and the two men hit it off immediately. Two years later, Crick and Watson solved the structure of DNA. They decided whose name should be first on their famous paper by flipping a coin. Crick went on to study how RNA works and was involved in the building of proteins inside cells. In 1961 he and Sydney Brenner proved that a triplet code—a codon—was the key to reading the information encoded on DNA. In 1976 Crick moved to the Salk Institute in California, where he conducted research on neurobiology. He died in 2004 at the age of eighty-eight.

**ROSALIND E. FRANKLIN (1920–1958)** Born in London, England, Rosalind Franklin knew by the time she was a teenager that she wanted to be a scientist. In 1938 she enrolled at Cambridge University to study chemistry. In 1947 Franklin went to work at a laboratory in France, where she learned the technique of studying molecular structure with X-ray diffraction. Four years later, Franklin began working with Maurice Wilkins at King's College in London. Wilkins, however, treated her more like an assistant than a colleague, and from the beginning, their professional relationship was very strained. In the months that followed, Franklin produced high-resolution images of crystallized DNA fibers using X-ray diffraction techniques. When Francis Crick saw Franklin's X-ray images (shown to him by Wilkins), he had the clues he and Watson needed to solve the structure of DNA. Franklin left Cambridge in 1953. Five years later she died of cancer, at the age of thirty-eight. It was not until years after her death that Rosalind Franklin was recognized for the role she played in discovering DNA structure.

**GREGOR JOHANN MENDEL (1822–1884)** Gregor Mendel is often called the father of modern genetics. Born in present-day Czech Republic, Mendel entered a monastery at aged twenty-one. He had a strong interest in natural history, physics, plants, and mathematics. In 1856 Mendel started experimenting with garden peas in an attempt to figure out how inherited traits are passed from generation to generation. Growing his plants in the monastery garden, Mendel carefully pollinated them, saved seeds to plant under controlled conditions, and meticulously analyzed the succeeding generations. Mendel published a paper in 1866 in which he concluded that heredity is transmitted through factors (now called genes). Mendel's work was brilliant but was almost completely ignored by other scientists of the day. In 1900, sixteen years after Mendel's death, three other scientists—Karl Correns (German), Hugo de Vries (Dutch), and

Erich Tschermak von Seysenegg (Austrian)—rediscovered his work. Working independently, they had reached the same conclusions about inherited traits.

**THOMAS HUNT MORGAN (1866–1945)** T. H. Morgan is known for establishing the chromosomal theory of inheritance. Born in Kentucky, Morgan loved the outdoors and natural history. In 1904 Morgan joined the staff at Columbia University and grew increasingly interested in species variation and how it came about. In 1911 he set up the famous "Fly Room" at Columbia. The room was cramped, dusty, and full of cockroaches, but the groundbreaking research on fruit flies *(Drosophila melanogaster)* that went on there changed the course of genetic research. Morgan and his students, including Alfred Sturtevant and others, provided the proof for the chromosomal theory of heredity, linked genes, and other important aspects of chromosome behavior. In 1933 Morgan was awarded the Nobel Prize in Medicine for his discoveries about chromosomes and inherited traits.

**JAMES D. WATSON (b. 1928)** Born in Chicago, Illinois, James Watson was an inquisitive child. He read voraciously, including the *World Almanac*. His great store of facts and figures eventually got him a chance to be a "Quiz Kid" on a popular radio program. He won one hundred dollars. At the age of fifteen, Watson enrolled at the University of Chicago. Afer getting his PhD from Indiana University in 1950, Watson headed for Great Britain to try to solve the structure of DNA. In 1953 he and Francis Crick solved the puzzle and built the first accurate model of a DNA molecule. In 1962 Watson shared the Nobel Prize in Physiology or Medicine with Crick and Maurice Wilkins. Watson went on to do research at Harvard University, becoming director of its Cold Spring Harbor Laboratory. From 1988 to 1992, Watson ran the Human Genome Project at the National Institutes of Health. An avid tennis player, Watson still tries to get in a game every day.

## SOURCE NOTES

46 J. D. Watson and F. H. C. Crick, "Molecular Structure of Nucleic Acids," *Nature,* April 25, 1953, http://www.nature.com/nature/dna50/watsoncrick.pdf (April 14, 2004).

## SELECTED BIBLIOGRAPHY

Alcamo, I. Edward. *DNA Technology: The Awesome Skill.* 2nd ed. San Diego: Harcourt/Academic Press, 2001.

Allen, Garland E. *Thomas Hunt Morgan: The Man and His Science.* Princeton, NJ: Princeton University Press, 1978.

Bryson, Bill. *A Short History of Nearly Everything.* New York: Broadway Books, 2003.

Henig, Robin Marantz. *The Monk in the Garden: The Lost and Found Genius of Gregor Mendel, the Father of Genetics.* Boston: Houghton Mifflin, 2000.

Lagerkvist, Ulf. *DNA Pioneers and Their Legacy.* New Haven, CT: Yale University Press, 1998.

## FURTHER READING

Arnold, Caroline. *Genetics: From Mendel to Gene Splicing.* New York: Franklin Watts, 1986.

Evans, J. Edward. *Charles Darwin: Revolutionary Biologist.* Minneapolis: Lerner Publications Company, 1993.

Fridell, Ron. *Decoding Life: Unraveling the Mysteries of the Genome.* Minneapolis: Lerner Publications Company, 2005.

Ridley, Matt: *Genome: The Autobiography of a Species in 23 Chapters.* New York: HarperCollins, 1999.

Seiple, Samantha, and Todd Seiple. *Mutants, Clones, and Killer Corn.* Minneapolis: Lerner Publications Company, 2005.

Snedden, Robert. *DNA & Genetic Engineering.* Chicago: Heinemann Library, 2003.

———. *The History of Genetics.* New York: Thomson Learning, 1995.

Watson, James D., and Andrew Berry. *DNA: The Secret of Life.* New York: Alfred A. Knopf, 2003.

# WEBSITES

*DNA from the Beginning*
http://www.dnaftb.org/dnaftb/
This animated website lets you explore the history of genetics in a delightfully fun, yet informative way.

*Genome News Network*
http://www.genomenewsnetwork.org
Discover the latest breaking news in the field of genetics.

*Guardian Unlimited Picture Gallery*
http://www.guardian.co.uk/gall/0,8542,627251,00.html
This site showcases a gallery of cloned animals and their stories.

*Human Genome Project Information*
http://www.ornl.gov/sci/techresources/Human_Genome/home.shtml
The official site of the Human Genome Project has links to many related sites of interest.

*Mendel's Milestone Paper* (in English)
http://www.mendelweb.org/Mendel.plain.html
Mendel's 1865 paper about his famous pea experiments is translated into English and annotated with links to more information.

"The Talking Glossary of Genetic Terms," *genome.gov: National Human Genome Research Institute*
http://www.genome.gov/10002096
Look up genetic terms in this online dictionary and listen to the experts explain what they mean.

# INDEX

## PHOTO ACKNOWLEDGMENTS

**The images in this book are used with permission of:**

© Chris Collins/CORBIS, p. 5; © Bettmann/CORBIS, p. 8; The Zoological Society of London, p. 18; © Lester V. Bergman/CORBIS, p. 24; © Carolina Biological/Visuals Unlimited, p. 30; © Lee D. Simon/Science Photo Library, p. 37; King's College London, p. 44; © A. Barrington Brown/Photo Researchers, Inc., p. 45; © CORBIS, p. 50; © Ted Thai/Time Life Pictures/Getty Images, p. 66.

Cover design by Tim Parlin.